Egypt
For Kids
People, Places and Cultures
Children Explore The World Books

SPEEDY
PUBLISHING

D1532786

Speedy Publishing LLC
40 E. Main St. #1156
Newark, DE 19711
www.speedypublishing.com

Let's learn some interesting facts about Egypt!

Egypt is officially known as the Arab Republic of Egypt.

In 2012, the population of Egypt was just over 83 million (83,688,164).

Mount Catherine is the highest mountain in Egypt, standing 2,629m high (8625 ft).

The Sahara and Libyan Desert make up most of the area of Egypt.

The longest river in the world, the Nile, runs through Egypt.

Egypt is home the Great Pyramid of Giza, one of the Seven Wonders of the Ancient World.

Egypt is famous for its ancient civilization, the Ancient Egyptians, who date back to around 3150 B.C.

The shape of ancient Egyptian pyramids is thought to have been inspired by the spreading rays of the sun.

Fly swatters made from giraffe tails were a popular fashion item in ancient Egypt.

The ancient Egyptians worshipped more than 1,000 different gods and goddesses. The most important god of all was Ra, the sun god.

The ancient Egyptians believed that the god Thoth invented writing and passed its secret to humans. His symbols were a bird called an ibis and a baboon.

The giant sphinx guarding the three pyramids of Giza is thought to represent the pharaoh Khafre (Chephren), son of Khufu. Sphinxes are generally believed to have been built to guard tombs.

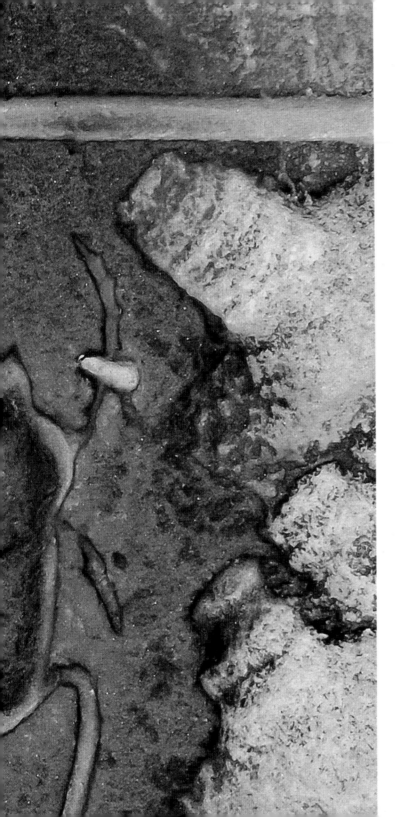

The scarab beetle was sacred to the Egyptians and represented life after death or resurrection.

Toilets were also included in some ancient Egyptian tombs.

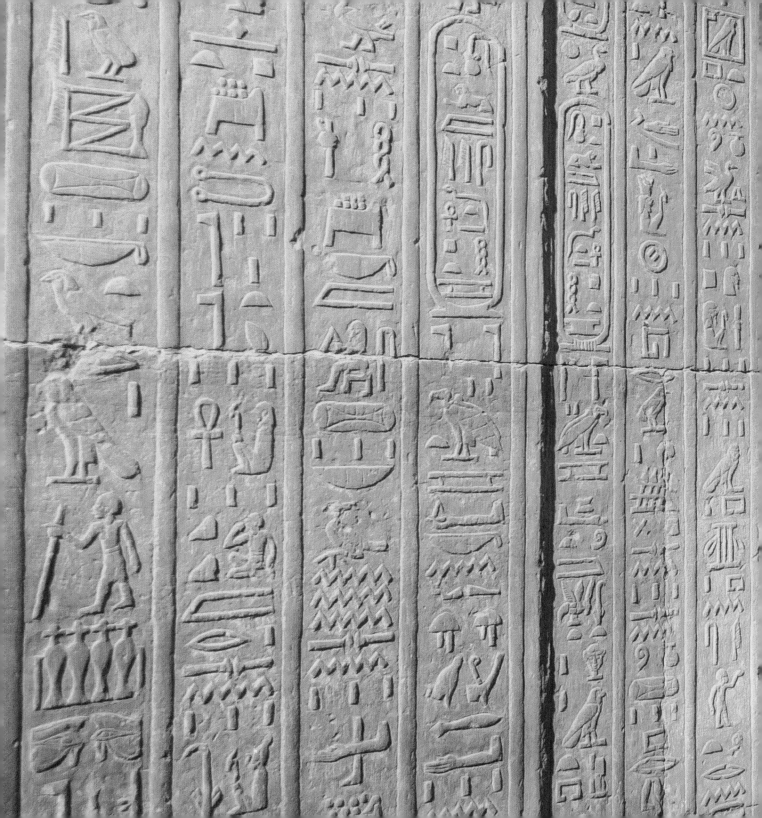

Egyptians invented scissors, toothpaste, potters wheel and the calendar.

Ancient Egyptian
Pharoahs never
let thier hair
be seen.

Ancient Egyptians believed the earth was flat and round.

Egypt has a lot to offer and you should visit the country soon and explore!